Unrequited

Unrequited

Poems

Patti Sirens

First U.S. edition April 2019

Editor and Publisher: Laura LeHew

Proofreaders: Quinton Hallett
Nancy Carol Moody

Cover Art: "untitled" © Jennifer Wildermuth Reyes
www.wildermuthreyesart.com

Copyright © 2019 Patti Sirens

Uttered Chaos
PO Box 50638
Eugene, OR 97405
www.utteredchaos.org

All Rights Reserved. Except for brief passages quoted in a newspaper, magazine, radio or television review, no portion of this book may be reproduced in any form or by any means, electronic or mechanical, including photocopying and recording, or by any information storage and retrieval system, without written permission from the Publisher. All rights to the works printed herein remain with the author.

ISBN: 978-0-9998334-4-5

To my Mermaid

CONTENTS

BLOWTORCH 1

THAT SPACE 2

AT THE CABRILLO MUSIC FESTIVAL 4

THE SUMMER DAY 6

ENTANGLED 9

NOT MY TRIBE 10

THE GOLDFISH 12

POMEGRANATE HEART 14

CAT MISSING 16

A SHORT HISTORY OF BIRDS 17

NOVEMBER 19

CROWS 21

WINTER 22

TODAY I DID 24

HOW TO PREPARE FOR THE BELOVED 26

BIOGRAPHY 31

ACKNOWLEDGMENTS 33

BLOWTORCH

in the small hours of New Year's
morning   1:39 to be exact
I saw my soon-to-be-ex lover
walking with her arm around
another woman
I spent that first day of the year
taking a blowtorch to everything
she gave me
reshaping the silver illusion
of where I stood in her life
obviously there was a waiting line
to spend time with her   I should have known
to take a number   but I was eager to think
I was her number one and only
and now that the blowtorch of my anger
has melted rebar and rearranged the
nuts and bolts of my assumptions
the whole affair a faulty
scaffolding careening towards
collapse
every memory of her
is a tin can on a fence
I am blasting holes through
and that empty space
is where the wind sings
halleluiah

THAT SPACE

between the breath   the rain
between the rain   the air

it's somewhere
in January   not a month
but a state of mind

two weeks and one day
three hundred and sixty hours
since I told her I couldn't
be lovers with her anymore

now
she's a memory
rattling around in the radiator
pipes of my dreams

each day
one grudging foot
in front of the other
trudges along
a high wire
that stretches
across
these silver months
between here
and gone   no safety
net   or escape hatch

the way I still
desire everything
it pains me to leave
is sometimes more than
I can stand   I reach

for her
for a smoke
a drink

find only
space
between
breath
and the rain

that huge nowhere is
everywhere now

I am here
and finally

I am learning how
to stay

AT THE CABRILLO MUSIC FESTIVAL

you shed your fuzzy green sweater
like an outer skin   I imagine
you unclothing   a lovely unveiling
our limbs and torsos twining
up the blue spine of an evening
what I mean to say is   I'm hiding
desire   wanting once again
what is just beyond my reach
to breach the humid air
between us
walking the invisible
high tension wire   I can feel
the hairs on your arms
a breath away   I want to
touch you   but don't
dare disturb the pleasant
being-with we share
there's an orchestra vibrating
the space we inhabit   I close my eyes
and let the music and your nearness
flow through me   my wanting
is a melody of horns and strings
an ocean pulsing
in and out of time   I want
to float on that sea with you
discover our songs and rhythms
when the beat of the drums
draws me out of reverie
I realize it's my own heart
playing its tympani
I long to be bold and impolite
take your hand
that's coiled around
the arm rest   reach up
touch your face
which is tilted
like a cat listening
to what is pleasing in the distance

break the silence of what's not said
in the shimmer of that music
kiss you on the mouth

THE SUMMER DAY
(with apologies to Mary Oliver)

this morning I woke
to feel you
gone   the electricity
not turned on
just the gas burner's
blue jellyfish flame
I resist the urge
to rest my palms
on that heat
to feel something
other than
numb   the summer sky
is impossibly blue
like a mood
or a vein
or the hem
of the robe of an
apparition   you've been
ghostly lately
wandering
through the halls
of my body
where I feel
empty   the memory
of your touch
is a hive of bees
under my skin
an itch where
I can't reach
to scratch   I pray
for a scrim of steel
colored air
the way farmers pray
for rain   you mirror
the storm clouds
inside me
the way ocean

mirrors sky
I don't feel
as vast or as open
but small and
contracted
like a star
imploded   the light
that reaches me
is an old story
of a heart
broken over
and over   I wonder
if the shallows I saw
when last I looked
into your eyes
are a mirror
of what I can't
seem to feel
anymore   the way
desire   reaches me
like the pale starlight
of an old story
turned to a myth
or untruth in its
telling   how many times
have I whispered
the words
cerulean   azure
ultramarine   indigo
when what I really
mean to say
is *I love you*
and even that
fades into
a color as drab
and ordinary
as wallpaper
that reflects the blue

jellyfish flame
of the gas burner
I resist the urge
to rest my palms on
since lately my hands have
been missing the heat
of your body
stretched over me
like the impossibly
blue sky of a languid
summer afternoon

ENTANGLED

Those two Mylar balloons
marooned
in the cherry tree
since the end of last summer
blending   at first
with the leaves   and then
the only thing
left
after the leaves   were
gone
the way their tangled presence
outlasted   us
after you
left
at the end of last summer
not even the winter storms
or wind   could
shake
that hapless nest
of plastic
out of the branches
which are
turning
full now
with pink blossoms
you are not coming back
though you are still what's
snared
around my heart
and I can't seem to
shake you out
of me

NOT MY TRIBE

I was a seed carried in the beak of a bird
dropped down the chimney of a strange family

not my tribe
though I looked like them

I had my father's short fuse and love for liquor
my mother's brittle bones   weak pulse and wiry figure

and not much else
my sister was the pretty one who wore the dress

she made the cheerleading squad and they were proud
I was their quiet dark cloud

I moved away
so as not to feel the loneliness

at twenty-seven I could have had
a baby   it would have been a monster

it would have grown up lonely
it would have moved away

instead I found a lover
and went to HER family

ten doves   nine cats   six rabbits   five parrots
a rat   a frog   a dog in a house of chaos

not my tribe either
I moved again so as not to feel the loneliness

and went to HER family   the one with the
wild-haired teenagers who played with knives

made crude bombs and fudge brownies
in the drafty kitchen   but I was only visiting

in any home I am only visiting
I am the gypsy without her caravan or dancing bear

where is my tribe?   where is my tribe?
my pomegranate seeds are dried

it's not about the U-Haul or the picket fence
but how you outfox the loneliness

it's my heart that wants a home   not a house
that's made of sticks   or one that's made of straw or bricks

I am the wolf blowing the whole fucking thing down
what's left are the crumbled bricks of the hearth

the burnt out tricks of the heart
the fire burning in the heart

THE GOLDFISH

I was thinking this morning
about the need to belong to
someone or something   some
   gang
   tribe
   church
   Elks club   or
   dysfunctional family
to call someone
   partner
   best friend
   millstone
   sweetie
   or even the person I love
   whom I wish I didn't
when I say belong to
I don't mean
   owned
   tethered
   dependent or
   beholden
but the heart knowing
it has a home and is free
to come and go at any time

in my meandering
this morning
past PetSmart
not yet open
I notice
someone has left a
   goldfish
in a jar of water
by the door
like the proverbial
   baby
left on the doorstep
of an orphanage

I almost lose it

in a fit of weeping   think
even that tiny golden
   speck
   in a bowl
needs something to
   belong to

POMEGRANATE HEART

When I think of you I think of a heart
   of pomegranate seeds   underworld   winter
rose petals spread all over the bed   wet spot
   and the windows of my body wide open
      letting in the rain

when I think of you   I think ravens
  and your black boots
the roots of your hair peppered
   with a tinsel of gray
      shaved close to the scalp

my skull against your clavicle
   the way I prayed the rosary
     of your bones beneath the scrolls
      of your skin
   trying to decipher the Morse code
   and ancient language
     of your heart

when I think of you I think
  of the coral reef of your spine
    and how I ran aground in the shallows
running my hands
   along all your sharp edges
     'til I bled and invited the sharks

teeth marks and salt trail
  along belly and thigh
sizzle of wires in the blood
   all my nerves in flames
     after a long and secret
       smolder in the walls of my body

the way you made my body electric
   live wire   lightning rod   third rail
my nails raking the skin of your back
   rowing the oars of your shoulder blades

'til we were so far from shore
   not even the North Star could reach us
when I think of you   I think of the RV
   broken down on I-5   stranded
      on a desert island of semitrucks
         and no way to get home

how everything went south after that
   the geese   the sun
      the yellow bird that broke its neck
         against the glass of a window
   trying to reach the warm nest
      of your hands

when I think of you   I think
   feather and fever
      sugar skulls and the smell
         of fermented apples
a season of being drunk on cider
   and the illusion of love

chemistry experiment in the basement
   gone awry   the foundation blown
      into a rubble of stone and metal
   a dust of false promise

when I think of you   I think of me
   running through a moonlit field
      of weeds   debris
         and night blooming flowers
spitting out pomegranate seeds
   blood red juice dripping down my chin

my barn owl heart beating its wings
   against the bones of its cage
finally setting itself free
   to fly alone into the orange light
      of a harvest moon

CAT MISSING

Sometimes I still look
for the gleam
of Sweet Pea's green collar
in the tall grass along the levee
hoping to find his bones
or what the coyotes left of him
vision of returning them
to Christine
who has long since
taken down the "missing" poster
with his photo on it
orange cat in a doorway
italics of her contact information
at what point do we let go
and stop looking for what's
gone missing
just listen to the crickets
in the early autumn dusk
coyotes yipping in the distance
surrender to that
strange new empty
space?

A SHORT HISTORY OF BIRDS

I listen to the delicate bones
  of her face   their minute shifting
    almost imperceptible at first
      like the stirring of wings
hummingbird I think   watching
  the sweat weave a string of pearls
    above her upper lip
then a great dark span
  as I touch the ice age
    on her shoulder blades
where she hides
  her raven wings

She has me on my belly
  I'm deep as ocean trenches
she loves anything that shows her
   surrender
she has climbed onto my back
   we are acrobats   Flying Wallendas
     falling in slow motion
twin souls
   holding up the world
we even looked like versions
   of each other
she with her riot of curls
  soft as a field of clover
me with hair red
  as cherry bark
the veins in her arms
   like cables
     the high wire we danced upon

Sometimes I can't decide
  if she is a man or a woman
she has me against a tree
  in the rain   she reaches in
I am deep soft loam
her fingers   scratching at roots

   draw blood
     smell of bark and sap
her lips are slippery
    taste of moss

I could always smell absence
   on her   bitter as autumn
     could see November in her eyes
even as I tap away
   at her edges
     I sense the sway of trees
   see all the birds
     take wing at once
I watch the delicate bones
   of her face   darken
    like a sky filled
      with a great migration
hear the cry of a caught bird
   great horned owl   or raven
     wing-clipped   preyed upon
realize it's coming   from the forest
  in my throat   I become
a flurry of wings
   careening through the trees
    bruising my hollow bones
     against the bedposts
she's looking down at me
   afraid to ask
      if she's the cause of all this

NOVEMBER

Sudden rain and the sound of a cigarette and desire snuffed out
a window closes in the small hours of the night
there's no keeping out the weather

did I tell you how much I hate November with its family history
of heart attacks and sudden deaths

I bang my shins on a sharp corner of something
I knew was there all along
rats are nesting in the foundation and the cat is no use

We were yowly in our lovemaking and woke the neighbors
the bed sheets sweaty and always wondering
if there would be a next time

there's a melted Snickers bar left over from Halloween
in my jacket pocket   where she hugged me goodbye
for the real last time

more rain heavy and insistent which sounds like something
hurrying towards completion
soon there will be reindeer on the roof and there's a darkness
in me that abhors celebration

I should be happy to be free at last
but I don't want that kind of freedom

I miss her weight pressing my bones into the longitude of the bed
we fell off the edge of the world and there's no way back this time
the maps shredded for rats' nests   the bridge washed out

I will remember how she always wore black and heavy boots
her hair smelled earthy of vanilla and roots
how I loved to kiss her but didn't trust her
not to break my heart

there was a knot in my gut from the beginning
unravelling towards a reluctant future

which is now as I write this on a stormy morning
in late November

the rain   the rats   my weeping making an awful yowling
the neighbors awakened and thinking
what the fuck is wrong with her?

CROWS

  everything
    sinking into their absence of light
black holes of the bird universe

harbingers of autumn
cornstalks
early frost

once outside of Sacramento   driving
  towards Yuba City
the sky darkened
 with an endless ebony dusk
   of wings

it was Christmas day
we couldn't count them there were too many
where were they going and why?

  their harsh call and response
the slick blue-black of them
   the universe collapsing
     into it

I keep saying I won't write about her again
  but I always do

WINTER

I want what is
   still winter
      root bound   hunkered down
hibernating
   in the mossy-walled lair
     between death and birth
the dreaming
   between the in breath
     out breath
       of the seasons

the early bloom of acacia
   too yellow   too soon
     against the brutally clear sky

she is not coming back this time

and that fact is a heavy jacket
   I've worn overlong
     wrapped around my skin
      too pale   too thin
       for sun
I want what's raw   blistered
   blasted open

I want to know
   the death of things
     intimately
those three days in the tomb
   the time of bloat
     and worm
   before the green fuse
     and bloom
that space
   where someone   something
     once was
       no longer is

I want to look
   into the face of
     empty   grief   and ending
to not flinch or look away

to run my fingers
   one last time
     along the cheek of who
       I so loved and lost
     to know that I was not
   the reason
     for her leaving
  watch her form
   receding
     into fallow field and frost
become the violet mist
   that rises
     from the frozen earth
then disappears

I want to walk
   through the open door
     between
       the in breath and out breath
       of the seasons
to stand
 in that terror
   of solitude and stillness

to shudder
   with the violent birthing

TODAY I DID

Today I did everything right:

>meditated when I woke up
>had one cup of coffee instead of four
>went to the gym
>walked an elderly friend's dog
>did laundry before going to work
>folded laundry after work
>worked on a poem
>cooked a healthy dinner
>chatted up my neighbors
>did not at all indulge in cigarettes or alcohol
>ate all my vegetables   flossed my teeth
>dotted my i's and crossed my t's

and still I feel like shit

maybe

>I'm in a spiritual crisis
>postmenopausal mayhem
>my brain is one can short of a six-pack of healthy chemicals
>I was born without the Happy gene

I feel no better
than when I've blown off everything
to sit in the garden all day   chain smoking
drinking beer or tequila   having weighed anchor
in the sea of I Don't Give a Fuck
intending to stay awhile   in the land of dirty dishes
mismatched socks   overflowing ashtrays
it's my party and I'll cry if I want to

or maybe it's just that I miss you
when thoughts of you sneak through the back door
of my safe routines and self-discipline
you are still the trouble I want to get into

when finally I sit still
and don't know what to do with my hands
having no match to strike
or cigarette to hold
no glass of spirits to lift to my lips
the way I no longer have
your hand to hold or your lips to kiss

maybe I just need to suck on something
stoking the fire in my lungs to keep me numb

anesthesia is easier
and I've always done things the hard way

so today I will place
one. foot. in. front. of. the. other.

each step takes me further away
from bad habits and desire

tomorrow I *will* do everything right
again
even if I feel like shit

the way I did everything right with you
except not leaving
when everything went wrong

HOW TO PREPARE FOR THE BELOVED

Put clean sheets on the bed wash all the dirty laundry from your heart

Sprinkle the bed with rose petals

Sage the house   light a dozen candles   adorn the room with Christmas lights and incense

Play all the music that makes you want to slow dance hip-to-hip
Play no sad songs or soundtracks from past relationships

Scour the bathroom sink   put out clean towels and an extra toothbrush   vacuum all the dirt from the carpet and dust from the corners gathered from past experiences   expect a magic carpet ride

Put fresh flowers on the table   ones that remind you of the soft and juicy parts of women

Prepare foods to feed your beloved with your fingers this may be messy   but in a good way   sushi   mangoes   papaya   pomegranates   oysters   and lots of chocolate   throw out the knives and forks and any pretense of politeness

Select a fine wine that sits thick and musty on the tongue   or a smoky tequila with salt on the rim   or tea hot and spicy made with ginger and cayenne

Remember that both you and your beloved are the dessert

Get rid of anything that has left a bad taste in your mouth   talking dirty is permitted

Rub your body with warm oil and greet your beloved with your skin flushed and hair still wet from the bath

Remember to laugh
no matter how nervous or awkward you may feel

Maneuver yourself or your beloved under the mistletoe   though you
need no excuse for a kiss

Remember you've been preparing for this   no matter the path you've
walked in the past

Remember that no matter how much you might fumble
all acts of love are sacred

Gift your beloved your heart and whole being
in present time

There is just this time   this lover   savor every flavor   every moment

Surrender   nothing lasts forever

BIOGRAPHY

Patti Sirens was born in New York City, raised by wolves and poets, and was a member of several punk-rock bands. She now lives in Santa Cruz, California, where she writes and surfs. She has survived earthquakes, car crashes and menopause, and is grateful to live near the ocean. She has led writing workshops, organized poetry readings, and was a founding member of Tribe Through Time, a women's spoken word performance group. Her first book of poetry, *Antarctica*, was published by Burning Bush Publications in 2000.

ACKNOWLEDGMENTS

Grateful acknowledgment is made to the editors of the following journals and presses for first publishing these poems or earlier versions of them:

"Crows" was published in *Tar Wolf Review*, Winter/Spring 2005.

"The Summer Day (with apologies to Mary Oliver)" was published in the *Monterey Bay Poetry Review*, Fall 2016.

COLOPHON

Titles for *Unrequited* are set in Lucida Sans. Designed by Kris Holmes and Charles Bigelow in 1993, the font is designed to support the most commonly used characters defined in digital typography.

The body text itself is set in Garamond. It is a serif typeface, named for sixteenth-century Parisian engraver Claude Garamond.

www.ingramcontent.com/pod-product-compliance
Lightning Source LLC
LaVergne TN
LVHW041238080426
835508LV00011B/1276